Food for Thought

Estee Lee

Presentation by *BookLeaf Publishing*

Web: www.bookleafpub.com

E-mail: info@bookleafpub.com

ISBN: 9789357440738

First edition 2023

For my kids

*There will always be a spot at my table for you,
even when you're grown.*

ACKNOWLEDGEMENT

With gratitude to:

- Ms. Chertorisky, my fifth grade teacher, who was the first person to ever recognize that I "had a spark" for writing. Fittingly, it was during the review and workshop of a poem I'd written

- Jim "Piles" Phillips, who encouraged me to keep writing when I thought I had nothing left in me after I was forced to give it up

- Michael, my loving partner, who asked— barely two months into dating— if I planned on writing anything new that wasn't work-related because he "wanted to read more."

PREFACE

Food is (supposed to be) a basic human right. In many parts of the world, it's often at the center of a people's civilization and culture: anything from social gatherings and daily sustenance to gifts and offerings. Our traditions are often shaped by food as much as the food is influenced by our response to what the world has to offer.

And, usually without knowing it, the very food we eat typically nourishes us in more ways than we recognize. The act of eating itself is a multi-sensory experience that can leave an irrevocable impression on us. For some of us, our relationship with food is a positive one; others, not so much.

Either way, food permeates our very being.

This collection is a mere fraction of the ways food makes up and impacts our lives.

Dim Sum (I)

Point
from the heart—

That's what it's
supposed
to mean.
Whatever
you desire.

Your choice.

I hesitate and
look around (but
not too obvious)
for a hint,
a confirmation:
the frown
the sigh— on a spectrum
the stare

like a mind reader
I assess and hope
I make

the right choice.

Bao

wrap and
envelope me
in your
warm embrace

strong enough
to hold
the sweet
the savory

gentle enough
to guard
the resilient
the crumbly

people assume
you're just
a tool
to ignore

My darling,
without you
I would
fall apart.

Half-Baked

We ran out of time.
the center isn't set
the edges nowhere near
golden brown

It's still raw.

Grief pours out of me
like half-baked batter
thick and indigestible.

the grief
it's still raw

Unsated

the hungry are not:
    a metric
    a quota
    a faceless monolith
lacking identity
stripped of humanity
robbed of dignity

spare me—
    convenience
    comfort
    distanced "charity"

a million—
    pounds of food
    packaged meals
    photo ops
cannot feed the hunger of
a starving soul

craving—
    authenticity
    care
    recognition
of our brethren
and their
incandescent personage.

Insatiable

You hungered

for food
    time
    recognition
    agency
    love

from your mother
    your father
    your siblings
    "friends"
    relatives
    the undeserving
    anyone

here
Hong Kong
San Francisco
Bend
Portland
Yelm
Sacramento
Los Angeles
San Diego

Mountain View
there

no matter where
there was always
us

and yet you always
wanted
more

Still
you hunger.

Dim Sum (II)

一 碟 || one plate:
anxiety
doubt
fear
curiosity
audacity

一 籠 || one bamboo steaming dish:
shame
anger
frustration
wisdom
courage

一 碗 || one bowl:
depression
trauma
guilt
empathy
grit

I am
this and
more

what the
world chose

and what
I chose
instead

the (dim)
sum of
me

K-Pop Kitchen Dance Party

Women
belong in the kitchen
they said.

Joke's on them.

Because in a
house
that was never my
home
the kitchen was
mine.

The kitchen
belonged to
me.

my sanctuary
my wizard's tower
my laboratory

In crafting sustenance
I sustained my

mind
voice
moves
spirit
creativity
identity

And
there was
nothing
you could do
to stop
me.

Remedies

be my
cha siu haw fun
ultimate comfort
food
against the
apathetic influenza of
our world

be my
instant ramen
expedient simplicity
against the
contrived & superficial
attempts at "deep & complex"

be my
chocolate chip cookie
childlike wonder
against the
made up rules of
adulthood

feed me
yes
but feed
all of me

Banana

look
looks like a duck
can't really talk like a duck
why can't you sound
more Chinese
don't you know
so-and-so's daughter and so
and so
goes to Chinese
school every weekend
and so
does Chinese dance
and so
is good at math
and so
is on the honor roll
   (so am I, actually...)

Are you sure you're
   Chinese
   Asian
   pretty
   smart
   cultured
   good

enough?

We are What We Eat

neighbors
let us celebrate when
We sit
down at the table
together
We stand
in solidarity and
We walk
the long road to
peace and equity

for We are
Mexican at breakfast
Peruvian for elevensies
Chinese for lunch
Japanese + English as a snack
Indian at dinner
French for dessert
with plans to be
Jamaican at brunch
Ethiopian at tea
Nepalese for supper
German for a nightcap

let us break bread
honor my/your/our roots
honor the ones who were here First
for We are
We are
We are

my country 'tis
of thee
of US

Dim Sum (III)

Snob.

too picky
too selective

who do you think
you are
how dare

you
bet your ass
I fucking dare.

I have seen
infinity cut down to size
a lifetime lived in the space of a mouse's sneeze

You fucking bet I dare.

I will cultivate
I will prune
I will set fire alight
I will burn away

anything/one
no longer nourishing these
mindfields

You fucking bet I dare.
I cannot afford not to.

Morsel of Knowledge

a mouthful of history
the flavors
shifting with every bite
bitter
sour
sharp
savory
sometimes sweet
rarely refreshing
hardly fulfilling

often heavy
the kind that coats your mouth
and won't go away
no matter much tea you drink

every once in a while
we are nourished
truly and completely
but
usually

we choke
on the consequences
and ramifications

the expectations

Rise

I was not bre(a)d for greatness.
I'll never be part of the upper crust.
My methods often go against the grain.

Even so
even so

I will always do what kneads to be done.

My spirit cannot be contained.
I cannot be kept down.
Like the sun dawning in the (y)east

I shall rise.

Slow Cook

There's no recipe.
it's tempting to just go and say
let's dump everything together but
let's take our time
let's savor this journey together

we'll follow each step even if they
don't exist and are, at best, arbitrary so
we'll follow our instincts references guides
They'll create a recipe of sorts.

Where's the wok so we can properly toast these
aromatics and see that
they'll bloom or else it
won't taste right? Regardless
it's all trial and error anyway and
we're figuring this out together.

What's next? no one knows but
isn't that the best part?
What'll we create?
What's to become of us as we evolve and change
and grow old?

We'll find out together. Yes,
let's figure it out together even if
it'll take the rest of our lives to do it.

Doughnut

It said so on my profile:
What would you get up early for?
Doughnuts.
Yes, with a period.
To show how serious I am (not).

You're not one for sweets, really
but that doesn't stop you from
adding technicolor sprinkles to my skies

I'd mention
glazes
icing
cream filling
but we'd just go off on a tangent
of innuendo dusted with
cinnamon-y laughs and powdered sugar giggles.

It's also why
you/we/I don't panic
when I say
I want a ring.

Food for Thought

Gather. We
Bring the ingredients. We
Prepare a feast. We
Stir fry traditions. We
Mix in personal flavors. We
Simmer and season until the memories
Are just right. We
Pepper in knowledge and wisdom. We
Fill bellies, yes, but also hearts and minds. We
Nourish the soul and body whole. We
Bequeath a civilization to our children. We
Show love through this table. We
Gather.

Lunchbox

What do I
have?

They can tell
they always do
What is
that?
Why don't you
have...?
Why can't you
be...?
Why are you so
different weird?

What do I
have?
An ancient people's
ingenuity and creativity
flavors and identity
edible
sustaining
strengthening me.

Yield

One for the
many—
two dozen
sixteen pieces
nine sections
ten slices

One act—
many steps
multiple bowls
an oven or two
a plethora of ingredients

One person to feed the
many.

A recipe
A method to give just
A little love.

Dessert

extra
unnecessary

a waste of money
and caloric budget

I
disagree.

My favorite meal of the day
is a reminder

unassuming
unintrusive

even the harshest mealtimes
can end with a little

sweetness
defiance